MW00999215

Sunbonnet Sue

❖ Visits Quilt in a Day ❖

by Eleanor Burns

To My First Playmates, Kathy, Patricia, Judy and Bruce

Published by Quilt in a Day, Inc.

1955 Diamond Street, San Marcos, Ca 92069

Copyright © 1992 by Eleanor Burns

First Printing, July, 1992

ISBN 0-922705-38-0

Illustrations, Debbie Smith

Photography, Wayne Norton

Printed in the United States of America on recycled paper. All rights reserved. No part of this material may be reproduced in any form or by any electronic or mechanical means, including information storage and retrieval systems, without permission in writing from the author.

Contents

History 4

From the Author 5

Fabric and Supplies 6

Yardage and Cutting Charts

    Baby Quilt 8

    Lap Quilt 9

    Twin Coverlet 10

    Double Coverlet 11

    Springtime Wallhanging 12

Cutting 13

Tracing 15

Sewing the Block 18

Removable Pattern Placement Sheets 23

Pressing 25

One Step Finishing 28

Sewing the Top 37

Finishing the Quilt 40

Springtime Wallhanging 45

Index 48

Sunbonnet History

Quiltmakers have instant recognition of the term Sunbonnet, a pattern known and enjoyed by several generations. But before these full dressed, youthful figures appeared as quilt designs, they were popular in the late 1800's as subjects for postcards, advertising, books and magazines.

The universal appeal of children busy at work and at play was captured by the illustrator Kate Greenaway at the turn of the century. Her designs in books and magazines brought these fanciful children into homes around the country. It was another artist, Bertha Corbett, who christened them with the name Sunbonnet, and declared that it wasn't necessary to show the face when displaying emotions. She illustrated the book, *Sunbonnet Babies*, which became the basis for the idea that quiltmakers now recognize.

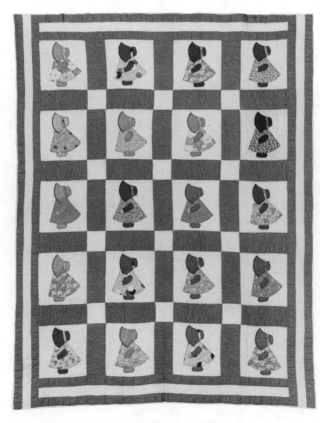

After the turn of the century, the popularity of the these figures as quilt patterns became apparent in needleart catalogs, magazines, and newspapers. For nearly a century imaginative quilt artists have challenged themselves to depict these busy children framed in quilt squares. With faces always concealed beneath bonnet or hat, these girls and boys continue to be the essence of childhood. They are each of us, yet all of us. They are the innocence of humankind.

Antique Sunbonnet Sue Quilt purchased by Eleanor Burns in Paducah, Kentucky, 1992

Quiltmaker Unknown

From the Author

My sisters were my first playmates....then came my baby brother, Bruce. How did he ever survive four doting older sisters! Somehow, peeping out from under a hat while we played, changed who we really were. Oh, the innocence of "Sunbonnets" at play on Grandview Avenue.

"Brucie" spent his days galloping about in his treasured Davy Crocket coonskin cap. Kathy was more the "Fortune Teller" type with her jewels and flowing silk scarves wrapped about her. A dotted clown outfit complete with a tall pompomed hat was Pat's favorite. Judy, with her Buster Brown haircut and bangs, always looked cute in her big sister's hand-me downs. I was quite dapper in my Annie Oakley hat and skirt, complete with rhinestones and fringe.

There was the capped baseball team, cheering in the side yard, the Doris Day paper dolls that took over our bedroom, and the grade school in the garage. *(I had to be the teacher, of course!)*

To preserve our innocence, Mother must have adhered to Bertha Corbett's advice: Never, ever spank the Sunbonnets.

How quickly my sisters and I moved into womanhood, simply by placing brimmed bonnets upon our heads with our stylish sack dresses. Oh, those wonderful memories to share!

In your quilt, may you piece together the bits of your wonderful childhood memories...those sunbonnet years!

Eleanor Burns
Eleanor Burns

The five Knoechel Playmates
Zelienople, Pennsylvania 1957
Back row: Patricia, Kathy and Eleanor
Front row: Bruce and Judy

Fabric and Supplies

"Reproduction" fabrics used throughout this book are manufactured by Marcus Bros. Textiles, Inc., from the Aunt Grace's Scrap Bag line.

Fabric

New lines of vintage inspired fabrics, based on the feed sack patterns of the 1930's, are now readily available in 45" widths. Quilts made with these cheerful reproduction fabrics in coordinated combinations duplicate those beautiful pastel quilts stitched from Grandma's scrapbag.

You may choose to purchase new, 100% cotton, "vintage" fabric, as well as add to the assortment from your collection of scraps. Include sentimental scrap pieces from children's clothing, or other treasured pieces.

Select a variety of fabrics in various scales of prints. Solids, small dots, and checks can also be used. The quiltmakers of the 1930's used the traditional small and medium flower prints, but added art nouveau designs as ovals to create a new look.

Often, the Sunbonnet's clothing was made from carefully coordinated calicos. Other times, a quiltmaker would select a favorite calico for the clothing, and coordinate one solid fabric for the hat, sleeve, and shoes. You may choose to use the same solid color throughout the quilt, or use a different solid coordinated to each outfit.

Fabrics can be from any color family in mediums or darks. For an authentic looking "depression" quilt, select pastels as pinks, blues, greens, yellows, and purples. While all fabrics should compliment each other, coordinate fabric in pairs. Lattice and cornerstones are made from an assortment of fabrics for a "scrappy" look.

Interfacing

Select non-woven light to medium weight iron-on interfacing. One side of the interfacing is smooth in texture while the other side has fusible dots. **Do not confuse this interfacing with paper backed webbed fusing.**

Supplies

- ☐ Fine permanent pen (light ink) for tracing
- ☐ Extra sharp dressmaker scissors
- ☐ Trimming scissors
- ☐ Pointer/turner
- ☐ Stiletto
- ☐ Extra long pins
- ☐ Safety pins
- ☐ Grapefruit spoon

Rotary Cutting Tools

- ☐ Industrial size rotary cutter with sharp blade
- ☐ 6" x 24" ruler
- ☐ 12 ½" Square Up ruler
- ☐ 18" x 24" gridded cutting mat

Optional Embellishments

- ☐ Narrow lace
- ☐ Tiny buttons
- ☐ Flowers or other decorative manufactured appliques
- ☐ Narrow ribbon
- ☐ Rickrack

Thread and Needle Selection

Sewing the Blocks and Quilt Together Use a good grade of neutral thread, and a #70, or size 11 needle.

Finishing Techniques Based on your type of sewing machine, select the appropriate thread and needle. The color of thread is your choice. However, many antique quilts were finished with black thread.

Sewing Machine with Straight Stitch Only

Extra Strong Thread for sewing buttons, carpets

Regular thread in matching color for bobbin

#90 or size 16 needle

A Decorative Chain Stitch can also be used for finishing the outside edge.

Embroidery floss to coordinate or contrast with fabric selection

Thread to match embroidery floss

Outline Machine Quilting

100% Cotton Quilting Thread

Machine with Zigzag or Blind Hem Stitch

100% Nylon Invisible Thread

Bobbin thread to match background

#70 or size 11 needle

Sewing Machine with Decorative Stitches

Black thread or thread to coordinate or contrast with fabric selection

Extra bobbins

#70 or size 11 needle

Hand Finishing

Embroidery floss to coordinate or contrast with fabric selection

Large-eyed hand sewing needle

Yardages
Baby Quilt
Nine Sunbonnet Blocks

Approximate Size: 37 $\frac{1}{2}$" x 37 $\frac{1}{2}$"

Background Squares
	1 yd	Cut (3) 10 $\frac{1}{2}$" x 44" strips into
		(9) 10 $\frac{1}{2}$" squares

Fabric for Hands
	$\frac{1}{8}$ yd	Cut (1) 1 $\frac{1}{2}$" x 20" strip

Fusible Non-woven Interfacing for Lightweight to Medium Fabric (Yardage based on 22" width)
	$\frac{7}{8}$ yd	Cut (3) 10" x 22" strips into
		(9) 7 $\frac{1}{4}$" x 10" pieces

Fabric Assortment
	(9) $\frac{1}{4}$ yd pieces	Cut from each $\frac{1}{4}$ yd piece for one block:

Sunbonnet Sue — Calico Dress, Hat, Sleeve, Shoe or Calico Dress Only* — (1) 7 $\frac{1}{4}$" x 10" piece or (1) 7 $\frac{1}{4}$" x 5" piece

or Suspender Sam
- Suspenders — (1) 1 $\frac{1}{2}$" x 3" strip
- Shirt — (1) 3" x 4" piece
- Hat, Pants, Sleeve, Shoe — (1) 7 $\frac{1}{4}$" x 8" piece

Lattice — (4) 2" x 10 $\frac{1}{2}$" strips
Cornerstones — (4) 2" squares

*(Optional) Solid Color for Sue's Hat, Sleeve, Shoe
	$\frac{1}{3}$ yd	Cut (2) 5" x 44" strips into
		(9) 5" x 7 $\frac{1}{4}$" pieces

Binding
	$\frac{1}{2}$ yd	Cut (4) 3" x 44" strips

Backing
	1 $\frac{1}{4}$ yds	

Lightweight Bonded Batting
	40" x 40"	Cut (9) 12 $\frac{1}{2}$" squares

Lap Quilt
Twelve Sunbonnet Blocks

Approximate Size: 37 $\frac{1}{2}$" x 50"

Background Squares		
	1 yd	Cut (3) 10 $\frac{1}{2}$" x 44" strips into
		(12) 10 $\frac{1}{2}$" squares

Fabric for Hands		
	$\frac{1}{8}$ yd	Cut (1) 1 $\frac{1}{2}$" x 26" strip

Fusible Non-woven Interfacing for Lightweight to Medium Fabric (Yardage based on 22" width)

	1 $\frac{1}{4}$ yds	Cut (4) 10" x 22" strips into
		(12) 7 $\frac{1}{4}$" x 10" pieces

Fabric Assortment		
	(12) $\frac{1}{4}$ yd pieces	Cut from each $\frac{1}{4}$ yd piece for one block:
Sunbonnet Sue	Calico Dress, Hat, Sleeve, Shoe or	(1) 7 $\frac{1}{4}$" x 10" piece or
	Calico Dress Only*	(1) 7 $\frac{1}{4}$" x 5" piece
or		
Suspender Sam	Suspenders	(1) 1 $\frac{1}{2}$" x 3" strip
	Shirt	(1) 3" x 4" piece
	Hat, Pants, Sleeve, Shoe	(1) 7 $\frac{1}{4}$" x 8" piece
Lattice		(4) 2" x 10 $\frac{1}{2}$" strips
Cornerstones		(4) 2" squares

*(Optional) Solid Color for Sue's Hat, Sleeve, Shoe

	$\frac{1}{3}$ yd	Cut (2) 5" x 44" strips into
		(12) 5" x 7 $\frac{1}{4}$" pieces

Binding		
	$\frac{5}{8}$ yd	Cut (5) 3" x 44" strips

Backing		
	1 $\frac{1}{2}$ yds	

Lightweight Bonded Batting		
	40" x 56"	Cut (12) 12 $\frac{1}{2}$" squares

Twin Coverlet
Thirty-five Sunbonnet Blocks

Approximate Size: 63" x 89"

Background Squares

2 $\frac{3}{4}$ yds	Cut (9) 10 $\frac{1}{2}$" x 44" strips into
	(35) 10 $\frac{1}{2}$" squares

Fabric for Hands

$\frac{1}{4}$ yd	Cut (2) 1 $\frac{1}{2}$" x 44" strips

Fusible Non-woven Interfacing for Lightweight to Medium Fabric (Yardage based on 22" width)

3 $\frac{1}{2}$ yds	Cut (12) 10" x 22" strips into
	(35) 7 $\frac{1}{4}$" x 10" pieces

Fabric Assortment

	(12) $\frac{5}{8}$ yd pieces	Cut from each $\frac{5}{8}$ yd piece for three blocks:
		(4) 2" x 44" strips into:
Lattice		(12) 2" x 10 $\frac{1}{2}$" strips and
Cornerstones		(12) 2" squares
Sunbonnet Sue	Calico Dress, Hat, Sleeve, Shoe or	(3) 7 $\frac{1}{4}$" x 10" pieces or
	Calico Dress Only*	(3) 7 $\frac{1}{4}$" x 5" pieces
or		
Suspender Sam	Suspenders	(3) 1 $\frac{1}{2}$" x 3" strips
	Shirt	(3) 3" x 4" pieces
	Hat, Pants, Sleeve, Shoe	(3) 7 $\frac{1}{4}$" x 8" pieces

*(Optional) Solid Color for Sue's Hat, Sleeve, Shoe

1 $\frac{1}{8}$ yds	Cut (7) 5" x 44" strips into
	(35) 5" x 7 $\frac{1}{4}$" pieces

Binding

1 yd	Cut (9) 3" x 44" strips

Backing

4 yds	Cut (2) equal pieces

Lightweight Bonded Batting

72" x 90"	Cut (35) 12 $\frac{1}{2}$" squares

Double Coverlet

Forty-two Sunbonnet Blocks

Approximate Size: 76" x 89"

Background Squares		
	3 $\frac{1}{2}$ yds	Cut (11) 10 $\frac{1}{2}$" x 44" strips into (42) 10 $\frac{1}{2}$" squares

Fabric for Hands		
	$\frac{1}{4}$ yd	Cut (3) 1 $\frac{1}{2}$" x 44" strips

Fusible Non-woven Interfacing for Lightweight to Medium Fabric (Yardage based on 22" width)		
	4 yds	Cut (14) 10" x 22" strips into (42) 7 $\frac{1}{4}$" x 10" pieces

Fabric Assortment

	(14) $\frac{5}{8}$ yd pieces	Cut from each $\frac{5}{8}$ yd piece for three blocks: (4) 2" x 44" strips into:
Lattice Cornerstones		(12) 2" x 10 $\frac{1}{2}$" strips and (12) 2" squares
Sunbonnet Sue	Calico Dress, Hat, Sleeve, Shoe or Calico Dress Only*	(3) 7 $\frac{1}{4}$" x 10" pieces or (3) 7 $\frac{1}{4}$" x 5" pieces
or Suspender Sam	Suspenders	(3) 1 $\frac{1}{2}$" x 3" strips
	Shirt	(3) 3" x 4" pieces
	Hat, Pants, Sleeve, Shoe	(3) 7 $\frac{1}{4}$" x 8" pieces

*(Optional) Solid Color for Sue's Hat, Sleeve, Shoe		
	1 $\frac{1}{3}$ yds	Cut (7) 5" x 44" strips into (42) 5" x 7 $\frac{1}{4}$" pieces

Binding		
	1 yd	Cut (10) 3" x 44" strips

Backing		
	5 yds	Cut (2) equal pieces

Lightweight Bonded Batting		
	81" x 96"	Cut (42) 12 $\frac{1}{2}$" squares

Springtime Wallhanging
Two Sunbonnet Blocks

Approximate Size: 18" x 32 $\frac{1}{2}$"

Sky Background

	$\frac{1}{4}$ yd	Cut (2) 9" x 12 $\frac{1}{2}$" rectangles

Grass Background

	$\frac{1}{8}$ yd	Cut (2) 4" x 12 $\frac{1}{2}$" rectangles

Fusible Non-woven Interfacing

	$\frac{1}{4}$ yd	Cut (2) 7 $\frac{1}{4}$" x 10" pieces

Fabric Assortment

Sunbonnet Sue		Hat	Cut (1) 4 $\frac{1}{2}$" x 5"
		Dress	Cut (1) 5 $\frac{1}{2}$" x 6 $\frac{1}{2}$"
		Shoe	Cut (1) 2" x 3"
		Sleeve	Cut (1) 2" x 3"
		Hand	Cut (1) 1 $\frac{1}{2}$" x 2"
		Ribbon	$\frac{1}{4}$ yd of $\frac{3}{8}$" wide
		Flower	(1) 1 $\frac{1}{2}$" x 6" strip medium
Suspender Sam		Hat	Cut (1) 5" x 6"
		Shirt	Cut (1) 3" x 4"
		Pants	Cut (1) 4" x 4"
		Shoe	Cut (1) 2" x 3 $\frac{1}{2}$"
		Sleeve	Cut (1) 2" x 3"
		Suspender	Cut (1) 1 $\frac{1}{2}$" x 3"
		Hand	Cut (1) 1 $\frac{1}{2}$" x 2"
4" Miniature Quilt		Part A	Cut (4) 1" x 16" strips medium/dark
		Part B	Cut (1) 2 $\frac{1}{2}$" x 16" strip
		Backing	Cut (1) 4 $\frac{1}{2}$" x 4 $\frac{1}{2}$"
		Popsicle stick	Cut (2) $\frac{3}{16}$" x $\frac{3}{4}$" pieces
		Wooden Beads	(2) $\frac{3}{16}$"
Flower Garden		Flowers	(2) 1 $\frac{1}{2}$" x 6" strips medium/dark
		Buttons	7 - 8 assorted
		Embroidery Floss	Green
Miniature Watering Can		(Optional)	$\frac{1}{2}$" x 1 $\frac{1}{2}$"

Borders and Backing

	1 yd	Cut (3) 3 $\frac{1}{2}$" x 44" strips

Binding

	$\frac{1}{3}$ yd	Cut (3) 3" x 44" strips

Lightweight Bonded Batting

20" x 36 "

Cutting

Cutting the Background Fabric

1. If the fabric is not on the straight-of-grain, make a nick in the selvage and tear from selvage to selvage.

2. Bring the selvage edges together, but match the torn edge.

3. Lay the folded fabric on the gridded cutting mat with most of it lying to the right of zero. Line up the torn, left edge slightly to the left of zero.

4. With the 6" x 24" ruler, trim at zero.

5. Cut 10 ½" x 44" strips.

6. Layer several folded 10 ½" strips on the gridded mat with the left selvage edges slightly to the left of zero. Trim at zero, removing the selvages and straightening at the same time. With the 12 ½" Square Up ruler, cut each strip into 10 ½" squares.

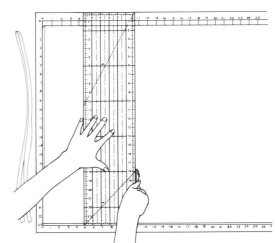

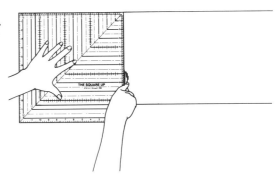

Cutting 1 ½" Strips for Hands

Cut 1 ½" strips from the fabric for the hands. Place the 1 ½" strips wrong side up on the cutting mat. Line up the quarter inch line on the 6" x 24" ruler with the edge of the strip. Lightly pencil a dashed line ¼" from the edge. Cut the 1 ½" strip into 2" pieces.

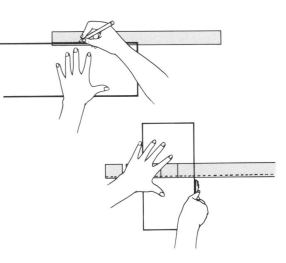

Cutting the Light to Medium Weight Non-woven Iron-on Interfacing

These instructions are based on 22"
wide interfacing. Cut into 10" strips
the width of the interfacing. Cut each
10" strip into three 7 ¼" pieces.

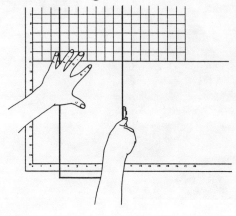

Cutting the 1/4 Yard and 5/8 Yard Pieces

Cut lattice and cornerstones **before** cutting the clothing. To cut the clothing, place the Square Up ruler in the lower left corner of the fabric. Cut the piece slightly larger than indicated, removing bruised or selvage edges. Turn the piece and cut to exact size.

Baby and Lap 1/4 Yard Piece

Cut one set of clothing for either
Sue or Sam for each Sunbonnet
block in your quilt.

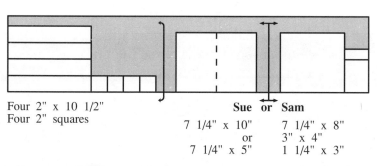

Four 2" x 10 1/2"
Four 2" squares

Sue or **Sam**

7 1/4" x 10"   7 1/4" x 8"
       or   3" x 4"
7 1/4" x 5"   1 1/4" x 3"

Twin and Double 5/8 Yard Piece

Cut three sets of clothing for
either Sue or Sam for each Sunbonnet block in your quilt.

Twelve 2" x 10 1/2"   Twelve 2" squares

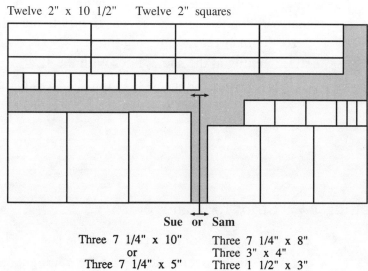

Sue or **Sam**

Three 7 1/4" x 10"   Three 7 1/4" x 8"
        or   Three 3" x 4"
Three 7 1/4" x 5"   Three 1 1/2" x 3"

(Optional) Cutting Solid Color for Sue's Hat, Sleeve, Shoe

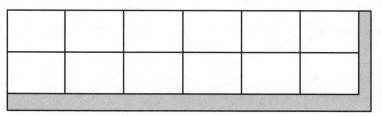

One 5" x 7 1/4" piece for each block

Tracing

Tracing the Pattern onto the Interfacing

Patterns are provided on the next two pages.

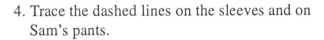

1. Feel the interfacing. Find the smooth side and the "dotted" side. The pattern is traced on the smooth side. The textured "dotted" side is the fusible side.

   Check the permanence of your pen by drawing on the smooth side of scrap interfacing and steam pressing the dotted side of interfacing to scrap fabric. Substitute pen if it "runs" when pressed.

2. Place the 7 ¼" x 10" piece of interfacing on top of the pattern sheet **with the smooth side up**.

3. Trace all pieces with a fine, permanent pen.

4. Trace the dashed lines on the sleeves and on Sam's pants.

Sue

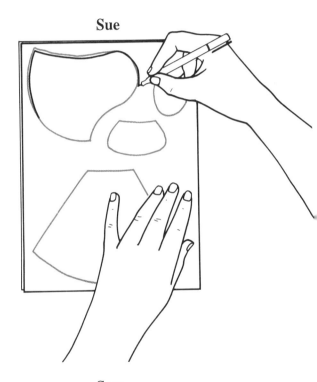

Sam

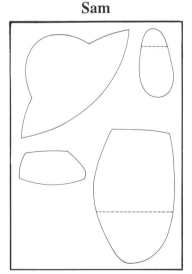

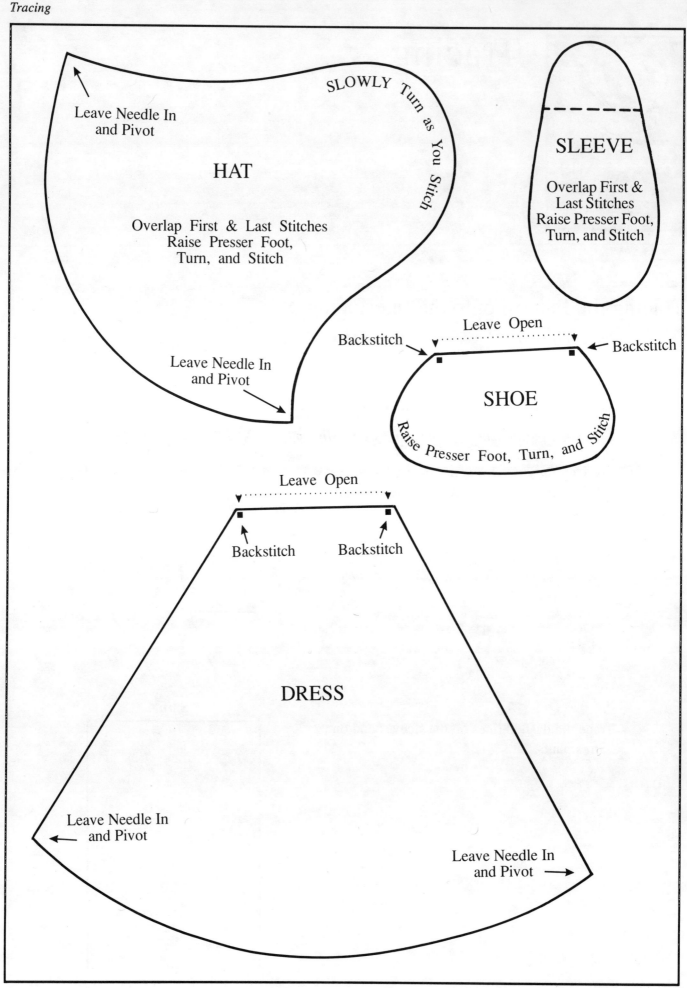

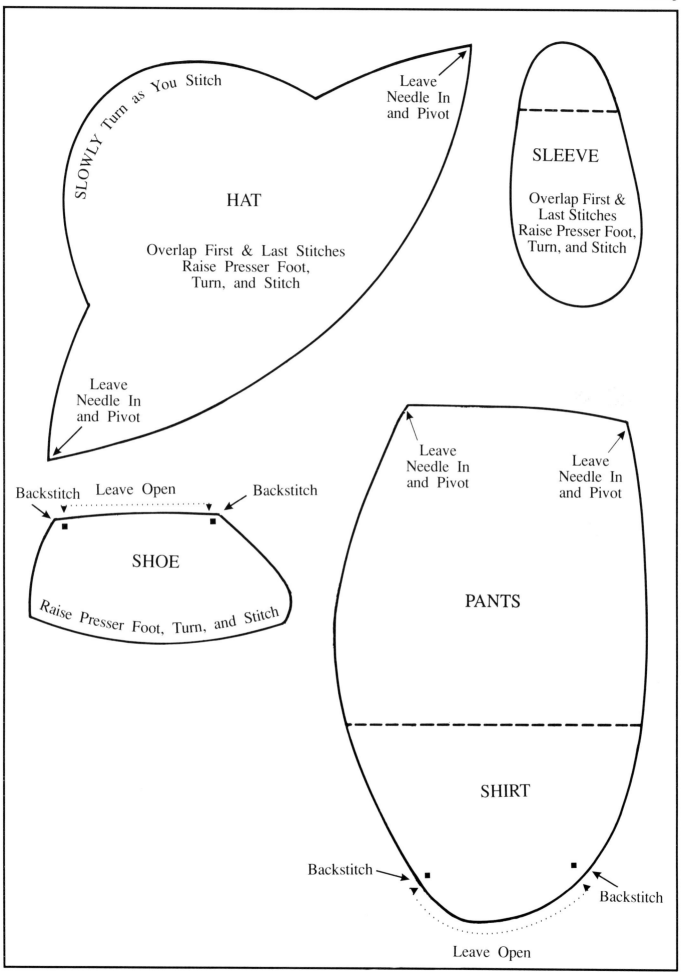

SLOWLY Turn as You Stitch

Leave
Needle In
and Pivot

HAT

Overlap First & Last Stitches
Raise Presser Foot,
Turn, and Stitch

SLEEVE

Overlap First &
Last Stitches
Raise Presser Foot,
Turn, and Stitch

Leave
Needle In
and Pivot

Backstitch   Leave Open   Backstitch

SHOE

Raise Presser Foot, Turn, and Stitch

Leave
Needle In
and Pivot

Leave
Needle In
and Pivot

PANTS

SHIRT

Backstitch

Backstitch

Leave Open

Sewing the Block

Sewing One Sunbonnet Block for the Wallhanging

This technique uses a variety of smaller pieces of fabrics for one block, which can be made into a pillow or wallhanging.

Scrap Clothing and Interfacing for One Block

1. Cut the interfacing apart by trimming ¼" from each traced pattern piece.

2. Make a stack of scrap pieces for the Sunbonnet as if you were color coordinating its outfit.
   Include a scrap piece for each article of clothing.

3. Sew a 1 ½" x 2" hand fabric to the end of a 2" x 3" sleeve fabric. Press the seam to the darker side.

   Suspender Sam: Sew a 3" x 4" shirt fabric to a 4" x 4" pants fabric. Press to the darker side.

4. Place each interfacing piece on each corresponding scrap piece with the **dotted side against the right side of the fabric. The smooth side is on the top.**

5. Line up the dashed lines on the interfacing with the seams on the sleeves and pants.
   DO NOT PRESS.

6. Skip to page 21.

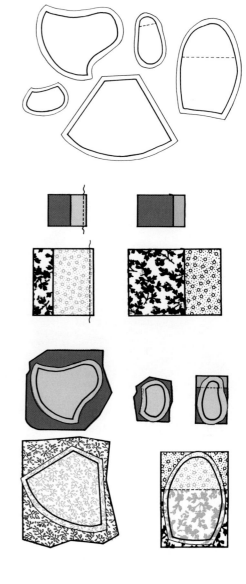

Assembly-line Sewing Multiple Sunbonnet Blocks for the Quilt

This technique shortens sewing time. A set of clothing is made from a piece of interfacing and fabric first. Then the sets are mixed, color coordinated, and appliqued to the background squares.

Preparing the Clothing Fabric for the Interfacing

Suspender Sam

Right sides together, assembly-line sew the 3" x 4" shirt fabric piece to the corner of the 7 $\frac{1}{4}$" x 8" piece with a $\frac{1}{4}$" seam.

Open and press flat.

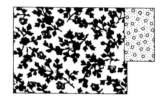

Sunbonnet Sue with Calico Dress, Hat, Sleeve, Shoe

Use the 7 $\frac{1}{4}$" x 10" calico dress piece.

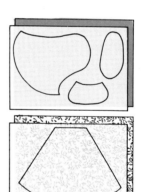

Sunbonnet Sue with Both Solid and Calico Clothing

Cut the interfacing in half. Use the hat piece with the 5" x 7 $\frac{1}{4}$" piece of solid colored fabric. Use the dress with the 5" x 7 $\frac{1}{4}$" piece of calico fabric.

1. Place the interfacing with the traced patterns on the fabric with the **"dotted" side against the right side of the fabric.** The smooth side is on the top.

   DO NOT PRESS.

   Sam - Line up the dashed line on the interfacing with the seam on the shirt.

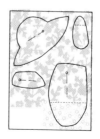 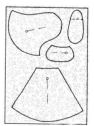

2. Pin in the center of the traced dress or pants, hat and shoe.

Adding the Muslin Hand on Sue or Sam

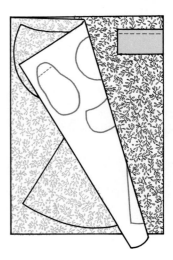

1. Flip back the corner of interfacing that has the sleeve traced on it.

2. Right sides together, position the 1 ½" x 2" hand fabric away from the edge of the clothing fabric with the dashed line on top.

3. Line up the dashed ¼" line on the hand with the dashed line on the interfacing. Flip the interfacing back to check the line placement.

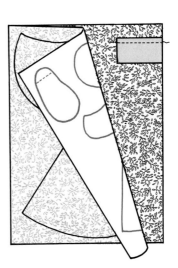

4. Pin in place. Repeat on all pieces.

5. With the interfacing folded back, assembly-line sew the hand fabric to the clothing fabric on the dashed line.

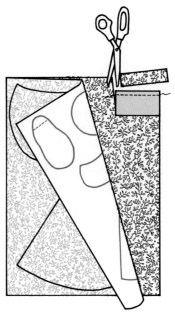

6. Trim away the clothing fabric.

7. Flip the hand fabric right side up.

8. Finger-press the seam behind the clothing fabric.

Setting Up Your Sewing Machine

1. Select a straight stitch.

2. Use the center needle position on your sewing machine.

3. Set your machine for a tight stitch, 20 stitches per inch, or #1 on machines with a setting from #1 to #4.

Sewing Around the Clothing Pieces

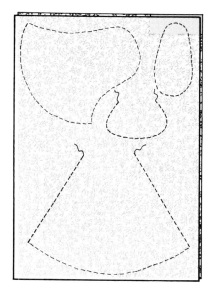

1. Sew **on the lines** around the pieces.

2. Follow the sewing instructions as indicated on each piece. Pages 16 - 17.

   If you used a thick, dark marker, stitch on the inside edge of the line, so the marker does not show in the finished block.

Trimming and Turning the Pieces

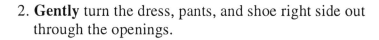

1. Cut the pieces apart. Trim each piece ⅛" outside the lines.

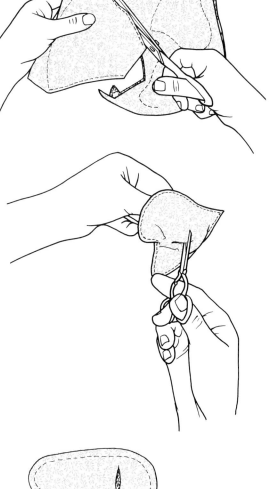

2. **Gently** turn the dress, pants, and shoe right side out through the openings.

3. On the hat and sleeve, gently pull the interfacing away from the fabric.

4. With the trimming scissors, cut an "x" in the hat interfacing.

5. Cut a **small slit** in the sleeve interfacing.

6. Gently turn right side out through the cuts.

7. Gently poke out the points, and smooth the curves with the pointer/turner tool.

8. Pull out the corners with a straight pin or stiletto. **Do not press.**

9. Stack the pieces, and set aside until all the clothing is sewn.

Making the Suspenders for Sam

1. Fold a 1 ½" x 3" piece of fabric lengthwise with right sides together so the edges meet in the center. Press flat.

2. Stitch across one end. Turn right side out.

3. On the opposite end, overlap the ends in the center slightly.

4. Press flat.

Coordinating the Sunbonnets

1. Separate the pieces into stacks according to your plan.

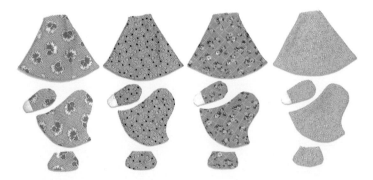

2. Mix and color coordinate each block.

Pattern Placement Sheet

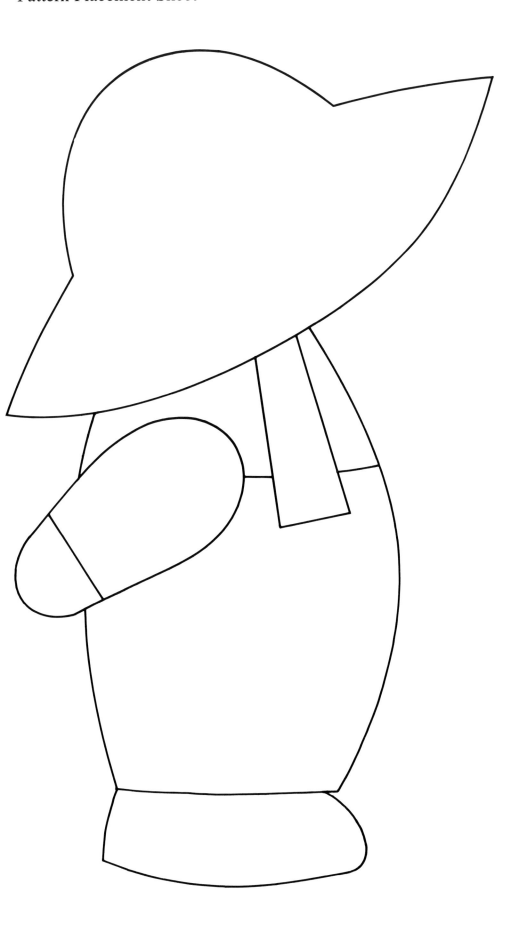

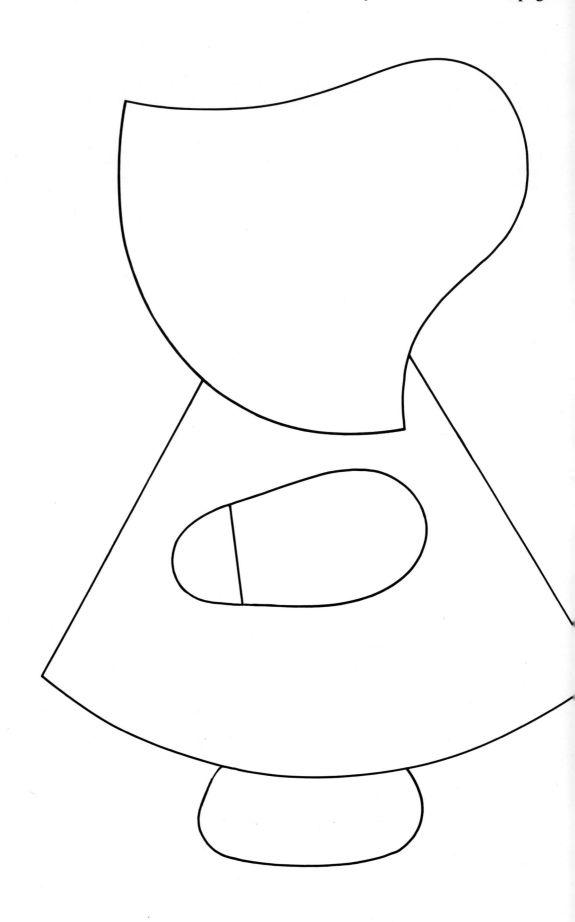

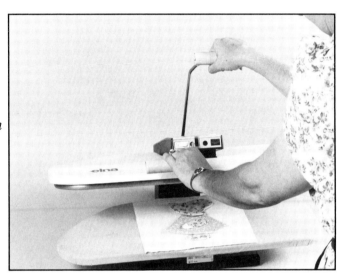

Pressing

Press the pieces in place with a hot steam iron or electronic press.

1. Center the desired pattern placement sheet on the ironing board or electronic press.

2. Center a 10 ½" background square on top of the paper.

3. Position the shoe on the background fabric, following the outline of the pattern underneath.

4. Position the dress, pants, hat, and sleeve in the same order. Fingerpress the interfacing under on the sleeve if necessary.

5. Tuck the raw edges of the suspenders under Sam's hat.

6. Remove the pattern placement sheet. Be careful not to touch the ink on the paper with the iron.

7. Firmly press in place to fuse the pieces to the background.

If you are not satisfied with the placement, pull the pieces away, reposition, and press again. If traced lines show around the edges of the sleeve, roll them under with the stiletto, and pin. The stitching will hold the edges under.

Optional: Twin and Double Quilts

See page 37 for "on point" placement of Sunbonnets on two bottom corner blocks.

ern Placement Sheet

Kite and Fish (Optional)

Use the same techniques of tracing the patterns on the smooth side of iron-on interfacing, placing the dotted side to the fabric, stitching on the line, trimming, and turning right side out.

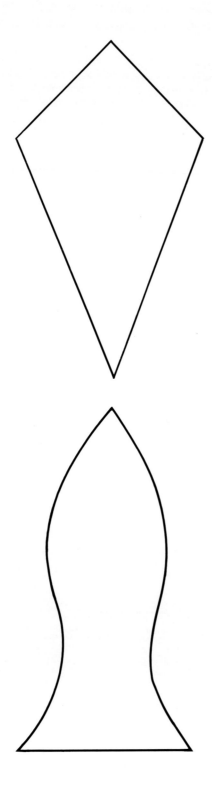

Different tilts on the hat and sleeve give character to the Sunbonnets. Add purchased appliques for interest.

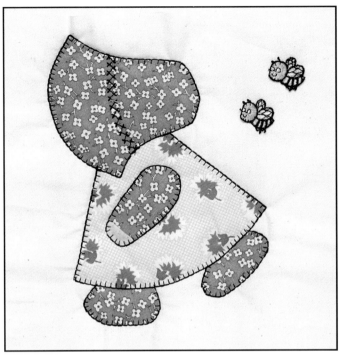

Stitch the kite string with a long stitch and heavy thread.

Make a second running shoe. The cross stitch on the hat was sewn on an Elna 9000 #110.
The blanket stitch is #120.

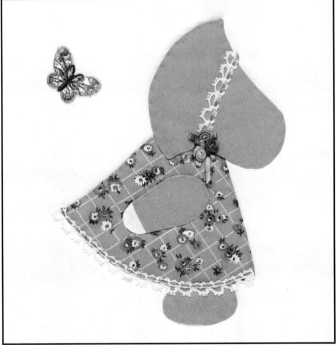

The fishing pole is a closed zigzag stitch with a stitch length of .3. Begin with a wide stitch of 5.0 and narrow to 1.8.

Embellish with lace, ribbon roses and appliques. The outside edges were finished with invisible thread and a blind hem stitch.

One Step Finishing

In one step, the block is layered on a 12 ½" square of batting, and the outside edges of the clothing are finished by machine. Edges can also be hand stitched. The backing is added in one piece after the blocks are finished and sewn together.

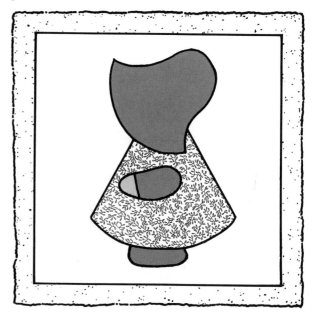

1. Cut the batting into 12 ½" squares with the Square Up ruler. Cut one for each block in your quilt. *Save a dull rotary blade for cutting batting quickly.*

2. **Center** the background square with the Sunbonnet on the batting. *If you plan to handstitch around the clothing, do not place the block on the batting until the handsewing is completed.* Pin in place.

Finishing the Outside Edges of Sunbonnet

Decide if you will decorate the Sunbonnets with Optional Embellishments. See next page. Then select one finishing technique based on your type of sewing machine. See samples on pages 30 and 31.

Try out stitches by sewing through a layer of fabric and scrap batting. As you experiment, pencil the stitch selection # or cam # by the stitches. Once you decide on a stitch, record its width and length.

Optional Embellishments

Embellishments, except buttons, should be completed before finishing the outside edges of the clothing. Use regular or invisible thread on the top and bobbin thread to match the background fabric, and a straight stitch.

1. Plan the embellishment.

2. Gently lift pressed edges with the stiletto, and slip the raw edges of lace or ribbon under the interfacing. Pin in place.

3. Stitch the embellishment in place with a straight stitch.

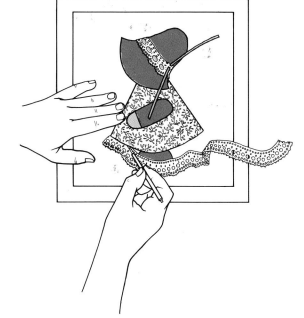

Cut a tiny piece of fabric, and hand-sew it to Sam's pants with exposed stitches. Embellish with manufactured appliques or tiny buttons.

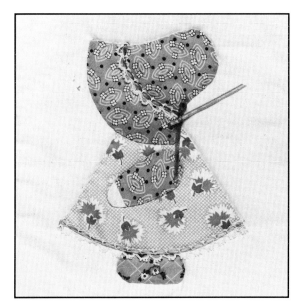

You need 12" of pregathered narrow lace to embellish the hem line and band of the sunbonnet. Remove the nylon tape from the pregathered lace before sewing it in place. Weave $1/16$" ribbon through lace and stitch in place. Stitch back and forth across an 8" piece of ribbon, and tie into a bow.

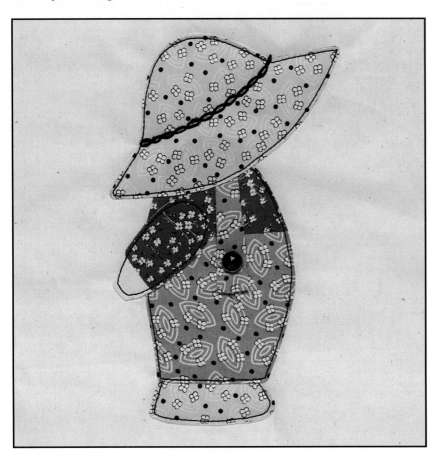

Straight Stitch Finish

Stitch used in example:

Elna 9000 #1

Stitch Length 3.1

Decorative Chain Stitch

Straight stitch plus 6 strands black embroidery floss

Fabrics used in example:

Aunt Grace's Scrap Bag
by Marcus Bros. Textiles, Inc.

Yellow 133T - Pattern 9515
Blue 122T - Pattern 9515
Red 111T - Pattern 9743

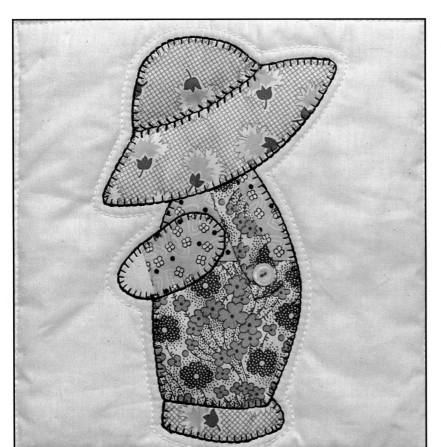

Machine Decorative Stitches

Stitch used in example:

Elna 9000 #120 (outside edge)

Stitch Width - 3.1

Stitch Length - 3.7

Elna 9000 #127 (hat decoration)

Stitch Width 7.0

Stitch Length 2.5

Fabrics used in example:

Aunt Grace's Scrap Bag
by Marcus Bros. Textiles, Inc.

Green hat 114T - Pattern 9518,
Green pants 114T - Pattern 9744,
Yellow shirt 133T - Pattern 9515

Blind Hem Finish with Invisible Thread

Stitch used in example:

Elna 9000 #11

Stitch Width 1.8

Stitch Length 2.5

Fabrics used in example:

Aunt Grace's Scrap Bag
by Marcus Bros. Textiles, Inc.

Pink hat 130T - Pattern 9518
Blue dress 122T - Pattern 9743
Pink shoes 130T - Pattern 9516

Hand Sewn Decorative Stitches

Block hand-sewn by the mother of Linda Amador, 1940's, Escondido, CA.

Running Stitch

(dress, shoes, sleeve, hat)

Blanket Stitch

(brim of hat)

Lazy Daisy

(hat)

French Knot

(center of lazy daisy)

Stem Stitch

(hat embellishment)

Sewing Machine with Straight Stitch

1. Set up your machine top thread with extra strong thread or embroidery thread and a #90, or size 16 needle.

2. Match the color of your regular bobbin thread with your top thread.

3. Set your stitch length to a long stitch, or a #4.

4. Line up the inside edge of the presser foot with the edge of a piece.

5. Stitch $\frac{1}{16}$" from the edge. Pull the thread to the wrong side, and knot.

6. Hand sew a button through all thicknesses to hold the suspenders in place.

Straight Stitch

Decorative Chain Stitch

Use this unique stitch, done with a straight stitch sewing machine and embroidery floss, to embellish the hat or clothing in any way you choose. Very narrow ribbon can be used in place of floss.

1. Plan where to embellish.

2. Cut a piece of floss twice as long plus several inches more than the area you wish to embellish. Include all six strands.

3. Match the thread to the embroidery floss.

4. Center the floss on the left end of the embellishment line.

5. Stitch back and forth over the floss to anchor it. If available, use the "needle in" feature on your sewing machine.

6. Hold the ends of the floss taut.

7. Take 3 machine stitches. Stop with the needle in the fabric.

8. Criss-cross the floss in front of the needle.

9. Take 3 machine stitches, crossing over the floss, stop with the needle in the fabric, and criss-cross the floss again.

Decorative Chain Stitch

10. Continue to stitch and criss-cross until the area is covered. Backstitch.

11. Leave long ends and tie in a bow, or pull to wrong side and knot.

Sewing Machine with Blind Hem or Zigzag Stitch

The blind hem stitch can "bite" to the left or right. A narrow zigzag stitch can also be used. With this technique, the stitches are "invisible."

1. Set up your machine with nylon invisible thread on the top. Loosen your top tension. Use a size 12, or #70 needle.

2. Load the bobbin with neutral thread to match the background square.

3. Set your stitch length at #2 or 15 stitches per inch and stitch width at 1 ½.

   If the stitch "bites" to the right, begin stitching on the left side of Sunbonnet.

   If the stitch "bites" to the left, begin stitching on the right side of Sunbonnet.

4. Position the needle so the straight stitches line up with the edge of Sunbonnet on the background fabric, and the blind hem catches the edge of Sunbonnet. The zigzag should catch both the fabric and the background.

5. At the end of each section, overlap the stitching, set your stitch width and length to "0", and stitch in place. Clip the threads.

6. Machine sew a small button to the suspenders.

   Lightly paste the button in position with a glue stick. Set the stitch length at 0, and the zigzag stitch width at 2. Hand turn the wheel to check that the needle hits the holes properly. Stitch in place.

Blind Hem Stitch*

Zigzag Stitch*

* Dark thread was substituted for invisible thread so stitches can be seen.

Sewing Machine with Decorative Stitches

The machine stitch that duplicates the look of antique, hand-sewn quilts is the blanket stitch. Depending on your type of machine, there may be other interesting stitches as the feather stitch or cross stitch, to finish the outside edge, as well as add a decorative touch to the hat or dress.

1. Select a coordinating or contrasting thread to outline Sunbonnet. Use regular or heavy thread in the top and regular thread in the bobbin.

2. Experiment with the blanket stitch, or another one you prefer.

3. Adjust the stitch so that the straight stitch lines up with Sunbonnet on the background fabric, and the "bite" is into the clothing.

   If the blanket stitch bites to the right, begin sewing on the left side of Sunbonnet.

   If the blanket stitch "bites" to the left, begin sewing on the right side of Sunbonnet. Some computerized sewing machines have the capability to "mirror" the stitch, and "bite" in the opposite direction.

4. At the corner take the bite. Leave the needle in, lift the presser foot, turn, and continue stitching.

5. Machine sew a small button to the suspenders.

Blanket Stitch

Feather Stitch

Cross Stitch

Hand Sewn Decorative Stitches

Several hand stitches are typically used to finish Sunbonnet edges. Use a long slender needle, size 7 or 8, and two or three strands of embroidery floss. Black floss was most often used in the quilts of the thirties. Knot the long end of the thread before you begin, and knot on the wrong side when finished. Use the sample as your guide, or create your own.

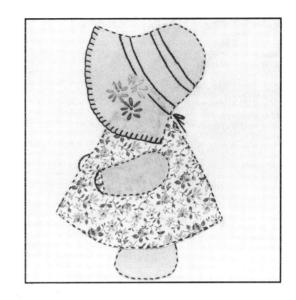

Running Stitch *Use this stitch to finish the edges of the shoes, sleeve, dress, and the back of the sunbonnet.*

Work from right to left, with the fabric edge between the thumb and index finger of the left hand. Weave the point of the needle in and out of the fabric five or six times before pulling the thread through. Make small even stitches.

Blanket Stitch *Use this stitch to finish the curved brim of the sunbonnet.*

Work from right to left, with the fabric edge between the thumb and index finger of the left hand. Hold the floss down with the thumb and insert the needle from the right side, catching the top edge of the sunbonnet. Then bring it out from under the edge and over the thread. Draw the floss through by pulling it toward you, forming the blanket stitch. Do not pull the floss taut.

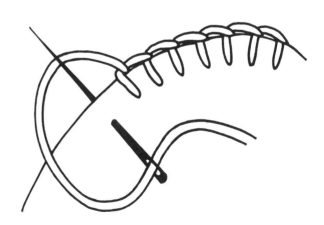

Lazy Daisy   *Embellish the sunbonnet with Lazy Daisies.*

Bring the needle up through the fabric at the center end of the petal. Loop the floss to the left. Insert the needle close to the point where the floss came out, and then bring it out over the floss at the opposite end of the petal. Insert the needle barely outside the petal loop and bring it out again at the center where the next petal begins. Do not pull the floss taut.

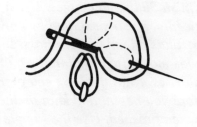

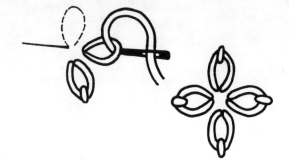

French Knot   *Place several in the center of the Lazy Daisy.*

Bring the needle up through the fabric at the point where the knot is to be made. Hold the needle close to the fabric and wind the thread two or three times around the point. Hold the floss taut around the needle and insert the needle through the fabric close to the point where the floss came out. Place your thumb over the knot to hold the twist in place and pull the floss through to the underside, bringing the knot snugly against the fabric.

Stem Stitch   *Use this stitch to embellish the sunbonnet.*

Work from left to right with the needle pointed to the left. Bring the needle up through the fabric from the underside. Make small back-stitches, overlapping each stitch slightly by bringing the needle out about $1/16$" behind the previous stitch. Hold the thread down with the thumb as you pull the floss through. Keep the floss below the needle as you insert it and bring it out on the line of the embellishment.

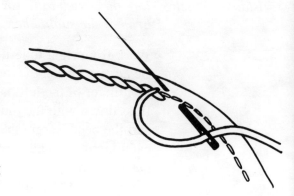

Sewing the Top

Color Coordinating the Blocks with Lattice and Cornerstones

1. Lay out all Sunbonnet blocks in rows and plan a pleasing color placement of the blocks within the quilt.

2. Color coordinate the lattice and cornerstones to the blocks. Mix the mediums and darks, as well as the scales of the prints. Avoid putting similar colors or the same fabrics next to each other.

Baby	3 x 3
Lap	3 x 4
Twin	5 x 7
Double	6 x 7

You may wish to turn the two outside rows on the twin and double, so the Sunbonnets "walk" around the outside edge of the quilt. When the quilt is on the bed, the Sunbonnets on the two sides are "standing." The two Sunbonnets "on point" are placed in the two bottom corners.

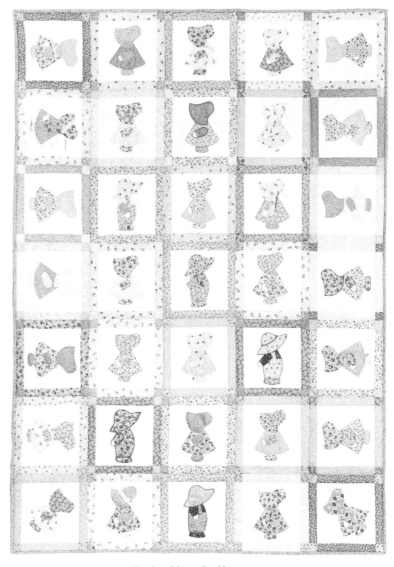

Twin Size Quilt

Sewing the Cornerstones to the Lattice

*Work on one coordinated block at a time. Use a ¼"
seam allowance and 15 stitches per inch.*

1. Assembly-line sew two cornerstones to the ends of
   two lattice.

2. Sew a cornerstone to each end of the third lattice.

3. Press the seams toward the lattice

4. Clip the connecting threads.

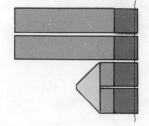

Sewing the Lattice to the Block

Change your stitch length to 10 stitches per inch.

1. Pin a plain lattice right sides together to one side of
   the block.

2. Stitch through all thicknesses. Fold back and flat.

3. Continuing around the block, pin-match and sew a
   lattice with one cornerstone attached.

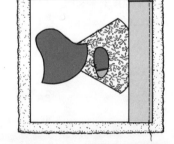

4. Pin-match and sew the second lattice with one
   cornerstone.

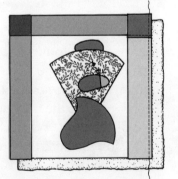

5. Sew the lattice with the two cornerstones attached.

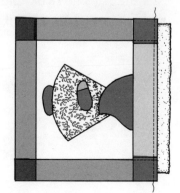

(Optional) Machine Quilting Around the Sunbonnets

1. Thread your machine with 100% cotton quilting thread, and matching regular thread in the bobbin. Use a #80 or 14 needle.

2. Set your stitch length to 10 stitches per inch.

3. Line up the edge of the presser foot with the edge of the Sunbonnet.

4. Outline stitch 1/4" from the Sunbonnets.

5. Pull the threads to the backside and knot off.

Sewing the Quilt Top Together

If necessary, flip the batting away from the outside edge.

1. Pin-match and sew the blocks together into rows.

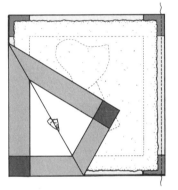

2. Pin-match and sew the rows together.

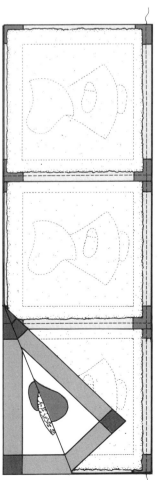

Finishing the Quilt

Preparing the Backing from 44" Wide Fabric

1. Following your Cutting Chart, fold the long backing crosswise and cut into equal pieces. If you custom fitted your quilt, you may need to adjust these measurements. If your backing is too narrow, use your leftover fabrics, and add a section down the middle. If your backing is too short, add a strip to the center or each end from leftovers.

2. Tear off the selvages and seam the backing pieces together.

3. Embroider your name and date on the backing with hand stitching or machine writing. Consider adding your state as many quilts travel across the country.

Adding the Backing

1. Stretch out the backing right side down on a large floor area or table. Tape down on a floor area or clamp onto a table with large binder clips.

2. Lay the "one step" quilted top right side up and centered on top of the backing. Completely smooth and stretch all layers until they are flat. Tape or clip securely.

Safety Pinning the Layers Together

Use 1" safety pins and a grapefruit spoon for quick and easy safety pinning.

1. Safety pin the corners of the blocks and the centers of the lattice.

   Grasp the opened pin in your right hand and the grapefruit spoon in your left hand. Push the pin through the three layers, and bring the tip of the pin back out. Just as the tip of the pin surfaces, catch the tip in the serrated edge of the spoon. Twist the side of the spoon up while pushing down on the pin, to close it.

2. Begin pinning in the center and work to the outside edges. Place the pins throughout the quilt away from where you will be machine quilting.

3. Remove clamps. Trim the backing to 2" on all sides.

"Stitching in the Ditch" Through the Lattice

1. Thread your machine with invisible thread in the top and regular thread in the bobbin to match the backing. Loosen the top tension, and lengthen your stitch to 8 - 10 stitches per inch, or a #4. Use a walking foot or even feed foot sewing machine attachment.

2. Roll the quilt tightly from the outside edge in toward the middle. Hold this roll with metal bicycle clips or pins.

3. Slide this roll into the keyhole of the sewing machine.

4. On the outside edge, place the needle in the depth of the seam between the two lattice.

5. Lock your threads with $\frac{1}{8}$" of tiny stitches when you begin and end your sewing.

6. Run your hand underneath to feel for puckers. Place your hands flat on the bed of the sewing machine as you stitch to the opposite side.

If puckering occurs, remove stitching by grasping the bobbin thread with a pin or tweezers and pull gently to expose the invisible thread. Touch the invisible thread stitches with the rotary cutter blade as you pull the bobbin thread free from the quilt.

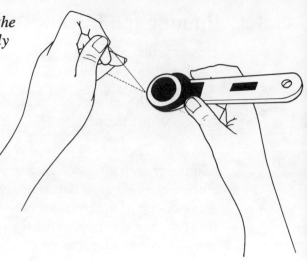

7. Unroll, roll, and machine quilt through all lattice.

8. Optional: Machine quilt ¼" from the lattice through all thicknesses.

9. Remove the safety pins.

Piecing the Binding Strips

1. Stack and square off the ends of each strip, trimming away the selvage edges.

2. Seam the strips into one long piece by assembly-line sewing. Lay the first strip right side up. Lay the second strip right sides to it. Backstitch, stitch the short ends together, and backstitch again.

3. Take the strip on the top and fold it so the right side is up.

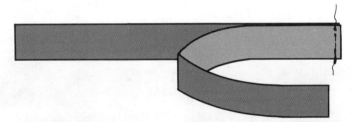

4. Place the third strip right sides to it, backstitch, stitch, and backstitch again.

5. Continue assembly-line sewing all the short ends together into one long piece.

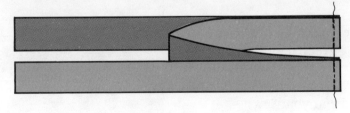

6. Clip the threads holding the strips together.

Adding the Binding

Use a walking foot attachment and regular thread on top and in the bobbin to match the binding. Use 10 stitches per inch. Batting is not in the binding.

1. Press the binding strip in half lengthwise with right sides out.

2. Line up the raw edges of the folded binding with the raw edge of the quilt in the middle of one side.

3. Begin stitching 4" from the end of the binding. Use a ¼" seam.

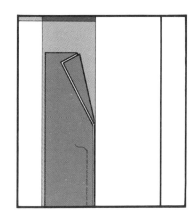

4. At the corner, stop the stitching ¼" from the edge with the needle in the fabric. Raise the presser foot and turn the quilt to the next side. Put the foot back down.

5. Stitch backwards ¼" to the edge of the binding, raise the foot, and pull the quilt forward slightly.

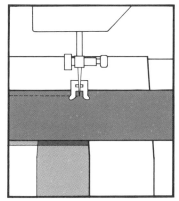

6. Fold the binding strip straight up on the diagonal. Fingerpress in the diagonal fold.

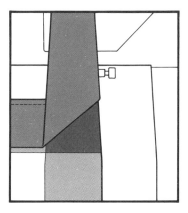

7. Fold the binding strip straight down with the diagonal fold underneath. Line up the top of the fold with the raw edge of the binding underneath.

8. Begin stitching from the corner.

9. Continue stitching and mitering the corners around the outside of the quilt.

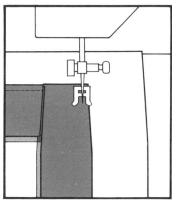

10. Stop stitching 4" from where the ends will overlap.

11. Line up the two ends of binding. Trim the excess with a ½" overlap.

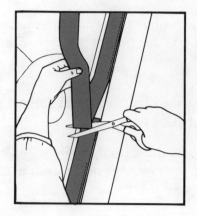

12. Open out the folded ends and pin right sides together. Sew a ¼" seam.

13. Continue to stitch the binding in place.

14. Trim the backing to the raw edges of the binding.

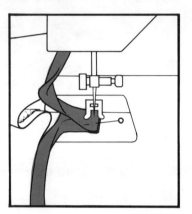

15. Fold the binding to the backside of the quilt. Pin in place so that the folded edge on the binding covers the stitching line. Tuck in the excess fabric at each miter on the diagonal.

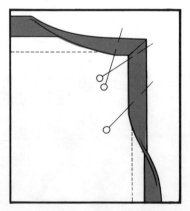

16. From the right side, "stitch in the ditch" using invisible thread on the right side, and a bobbin thread to match the binding on the back side. Catch the folded edge of the binding on the back side with the stitching.

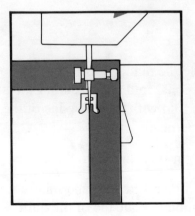

Springtime Wallhanging

Making Sue and Sam

Sew the pieces for one Sue and one Sam, following the instructions beginning on page 15.

Making Sue's Miniature Quilt

1. Sew the 1" Part A strips together with a 1/4" seam allowance and 15 stitches per inch.

2. Press the seams to one side.

3. Measure the width of the Part A strips. Trim back the Part B strip to that width.

4. Pin the two strips right sides together. Sew the two long sides.

5. At the right end of the sewn strips, lay the ruler pointing upward to get an even triangular piece. Cut along both sides of the ruler.

6. Reposition the ruler, and cut a total of four triangles.

7. Open the triangles at the tip by removing the stitches. Press seams toward B. Square to the same size.

8. Lay out the four blocks and sew together. Press.

9. Right sides together, pin the backing to the miniature quilt top.

10. Sew around three sides, turn right side out, and hand stitch the opening closed.

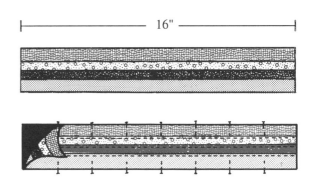

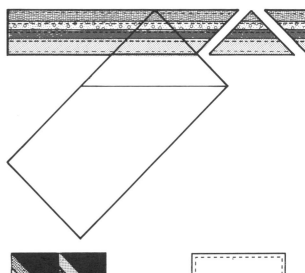

Making Flowers

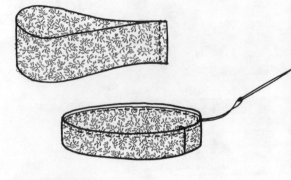

1. Fold strips right sides together. Machine sew along the short ends, turning the strips into rings.

2. Fold the rings in half, right sides out, with raw edges matching.

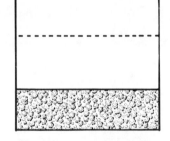

3. With double thread, run a hand basting stitch around the raw edges. Pull tight and knot. Using the same thread, sew a button to the center of the flower. Set aside until the background is finished.

Finishing the Blocks

1. Sew the grass to the sky. Press the seams to the darker side.

2. Measure 3 1/2" down from the top on one. Lightly draw a clothesline. Machine sew on the line with the decorative chain stitch (page 32) or hand stitch on the line with the running stitch (page 35) or stem stitch (page 36).

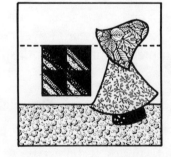

3. Following the photograph, position Sue to the right on her block, and Sam to the left on his block. Save the sleeves for after the decorations are completed.

4. Press in place.

5. Finish the outside edges of the Sunbonnets as you choose. (Pages 28 -33)

6. Hand sew the top of the quilt onto the clothesline 1 1/2" in from the left edge of the quilt.

7. Glue the clothespins onto the ends of the quilt.

Clothespins: Cut off the ends of a popsicle stick with a knife. Glue tiny wooden beads to the tops.

8. Flower Garden: Following the design on the photograph, stitch the stems and the leaves with the lazy daisy stitch (page 36).

9. Sew the buttons and flowers in place.

Finishing the Wallhanging

1. Sew a 3 1/2" border between the two blocks. Square off the ends.

2. Pin and sew borders to the two long sides. Square off the ends.

3. Sew borders to the top and bottom. Square off the ends.

4. Finish the wallhanging with machine quilting and binding. (pages 40-44)

5. With the sleeve unattached, finish the edges. Hand stitch in position, following the photograph.

6. Optional: Stitch a watering can in Sam's hand.

Springtime Wallhanging

Acknowledgments

Front Cover

In June, 1992, each student attending the Teacher Training Seminar at Quilt in a Day made a Sunbonnet from Aunt Grace's Scrap Bag, a line of fabric manufactured by Marcus Brothers Textiles, Inc. Eleanor duplicated the look of handwork by finishing the outside edges of each block on her Elna 9000. Using "reproduction" fabrics and modern machine technology, the quilt captures the charm of the 30's quilts.

Back Cover

Quilt in a Day celebrated the arrival of McKenna Williams, born May 2, 1992, with a new twin size Sunbonnet quilt. Each staff member made and proudly presented a block to Karen, McKenna's mother, a Quilt in a Day telemarketing representative. The Sunbonnets are perfect blocks for a "team" baby shower quilt.

Index

Baby Quilt	8	Lattice	37,38
Backing	40	Lazy Daisy	36
Batting	28		
Binding	42,43,44	Machine Quilting	39
Blanket Stitch	35	Multiple Sunbonnets	19--22
Blind Hem Finish	31,33	One Step Finishing	28
Block Layout	25,37		
		Pattern Pieces	16,17
Cornerstones	37,38	Pattern Placement Sheet	23,24
Cutting	13,14	Pressing	25
Decorative Chain Stitch	30,32	Running Stitch	35
Decorative Stitching	30,34		
Different Tilts	27	Safety Pinning	41
Double Coverlet	11	Scrap Sunbonnets	18
		Springtime Wallhanging	12,45--47
Embellishments	29	Stem Stitch	36
		"Stitching in the Ditch"	41
Fabric	6	Straight Stitch	30,32
French Knot	36	Supplies	7
Hand Sewn Decorative Stitches	31,35	Tracing	15
History	4	Twin Coverlet	10
Iron-on Interfacing	6,18,19	Zigzag Stitch	33
Invisible Thread	31		
Lap Quilt	9		